LIFE ALONG THE
RIVER
NILE

JANE SHUTER

First published in Great Britain by Heinemann Library,
Halley Court, Jordan Hill, Oxford
OX2 8EJ, part of Harcourt Education.
Heinemann is a registered trademark of Harcourt
Education Ltd.

© Harcourt Education Ltd 2005
First published in paperback in 2006
The moral right of the proprietor has been asserted.

Produced for Heinemann Library by
    Bender Richardson White
Editor: Lionel Bender, Nancy Dickmann, Tanvi Rai
Designer and Media Conversion: Ben White and
    Ron Kamen
Illustrations: John James, Jonathon Adams and
    Jeff Edwards
Maps: Stefan Chabluk
Picture Researcher: Cathy Stastny and
    Maria Joannou
Production Controller: Kim Richardson and
    Séverine Ribierre

Originated by Ambassador Litho Ltd
Printed in China

ISBN 0 431 113033 (hardback)
09 08 07 06 05
10 9 8 7 6 5 4 3 2 1

ISBN 0 431 113114 (paperback)
10 09 08 07 06
10 9 8 7 6 5 4 3 2 1

British Library Cataloguing in Publication Data
Shuter, Jane
  Life along the River Nile. - (Picture the past)
  932
A full catalogue record for this book is available
from the British Library.

Acknowledgements:
The publishers would like to thank the following for
permission to reproduce photographs: Ancient Art
and Architecture/John P. Stevens p. **13**; Ancient Art
and Architecture/R. Sheridan pp. **9**, **11**, **19**;
Heinemann Library pp. **10**, **14**; Peter Evans p. **30**; Phil
Cooke/Magnet Harlequin p. **6**; Photo Archive p. **23**;
Trustees of the British Museum, London pp. **16**, **20**,
26, **28** (numbers 821-PS337236, EA2560-PS239457,
EA9901/5-PS290776, EA4157-PS330979); Werner
Forman Archive/Dr E. Strouhal pp. **12**, **21**, **25**; Werner
Forman Archive/British Museum, London pp. **8**, **18**,
27 (numbers PH2638a, PH2843, PH1044); Werner
Forman Archive/Shimmel Collection, New York p. **24**.

Cover photograph of a painting in the tomb of Ipy
depicting fishermen casting their net reproduced
with permission of Werner Forman Archive.

Every effort has been made to contact copyright
holders of any material reproduced in this book. Any
omissions will be rectified in subsequent printings if
notice is given to the publishers.

Any words appearing in bold, **like this**, are
explained in the Glossary.

www.heinemann.co.uk/library
Visit our website to find out more information
about **Heinemann Library** books.

To order:
☎ Phone 44 (0) 1865 888066
🖹 Send a fax to 44 (0) 1865 314091
   Visit the Heinemann Bookshop at
💻 www.heinemann.co.uk/library to browse our
   catalogue and order online.

ABOUT THIS BOOK

This book is about daily life in towns
and villages along the River Nile in
ancient Egyptian times. The ancient
Egyptian civilization lasted from
about 3100 BC to 30 BC. The Nile
runs the whole length of Egypt, and
the country grew up around it. Most
of Egypt is desert. There is very little
rain. People depended on the river
for food, drinking water, water to
wash and cook with, and transport.
Almost everyone lived and farmed
along the river. Sailing along the
Nile was the only way people could
get from one end of the country to
the other.

We have illustrated this book with
photographs of objects from ancient
Egyptian times and artists' ideas of
town life then. These drawings are
based on information that has been
found by **archaeologists**.

The author
Jane Shuter is a professional writer and editor
of non-fiction books for children. She
graduated from Lancaster University in 1976
with a BA honours degree and then earned a
teaching qualification. She taught from 1976
to 1983, changing to editing and writing when
her son was born. She lives in Oxford with her
husband and son.

Contents

The River Nile

The ancient Egyptians lived and farmed along the River Nile, using the soil to produce food for themselves and their animals. In ancient times, the Nile flooded each year from July to October. When the water went down, it left behind lots of mud that became a rich soil that **crops** grew well in. The Egyptians used the river for water and for the fish and wild birds living on it. The Nile was also the quickest and easiest way to travel around. The **pharaoh** used the Nile to send **officials** or soldiers to all parts of his kingdom.

Look for these:
The model of a boat shows you the subject of each double-page chapter in the book. The picture of a scribe shows you boxes with interesting facts and figures about life along the Nile in ancient Egyptian times.

TIMELINE OF EVENTS IN THIS BOOK

3100 BC Egypt is ruled by one ruler for the first time. The pharaoh has four officials to help him rule, each one living in a different town along the River Nile.

2400 BC Uni, official of the land around Aswan, has a canal built from Aswan to the waterfalls at Elephantine. The ancient Egyptians can sail further south than before.

| EARLY PERIOD 3100–2686 BC | OLD KINGDOM 2686–2181 BC | | MIDDLE KINGDOM 2055–1650 BC | |

3000 BC   2500 BC   2000 BC   1500 BC

During the Early Period and Old Kingdom pharaohs rule from Memphis.

During the Middle and New Kingdoms pharaohs rule mostly from the town of Thebes.

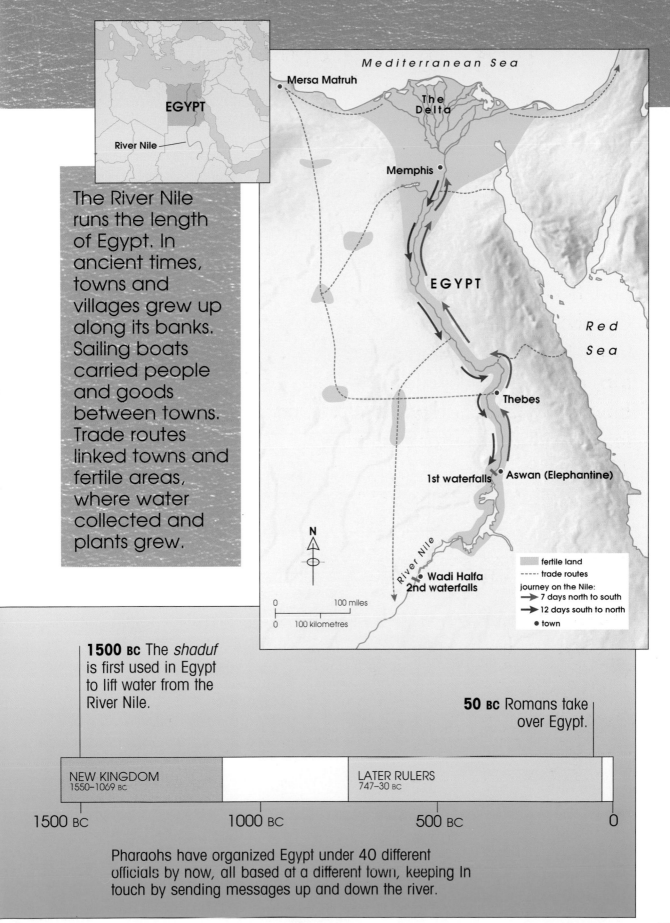

The River Nile runs the length of Egypt. In ancient times, towns and villages grew up along its banks. Sailing boats carried people and goods between towns. Trade routes linked towns and fertile areas, where water collected and plants grew.

EGYPT

River Nile

Mediterranean Sea

Mersa Matruh

The Delta

Memphis

EGYPT

Red Sea

Thebes

1st waterfalls

Aswan (Elephantine)

N

River Nile

Wadi Halfa
2nd waterfalls

0   100 miles
0   100 kilometres

▢ fertile land
---- trade routes
journey on the Nile:
→ 7 days north to south
➔ 12 days south to north
● town

1500 BC The *shaduf* is first used in Egypt to lift water from the River Nile.

50 BC Romans take over Egypt.

| NEW KINGDOM 1550–1069 BC | | LATER RULERS 747–30 BC | |

1500 BC   1000 BC   500 BC   0

Pharaohs have organized Egypt under 40 different officials by now, all based at a different town, keeping in touch by sending messages up and down the river.

Beside the river

The ancient Egyptians could grow **crops** only in the mud left behind when the Nile flooded. So they had fields all along the River Nile. Towns and villages were scattered along the edges of the fields, just above flood level. Most villagers were farmers. Farmers lived in towns, too, along with craftworkers, **traders** and other workers and their families.

HAPY, RIVER GOD

An ancient Egyptian song to Hapy, god of the River Nile, says how important the river is: 'He is father of the barley and the wheat. If he is slow to rise, people hold their breath then grow fierce as food runs out. When he rises well, the people and the land rejoice.'

As in ancient times, many Egyptian farmers use a *shaduf*, a pole with a bucket at one end and a weight on the other (in this picture not attached yet) to lift water from the River Nile.

The mud that the Nile left behind needed lots of watering. The ancient Egyptians tried to trap as much floodwater as possible, so they did not have to constantly get water from the river. Each year they mended the mud-brick **reservoirs** that they built to trap and hold floodwater. They also had a network of **irrigation canals** that filled with water during the flood and were refilled from the reservoir.

This picture shows how the water was carried around the fields in canals.
Canals had:
- wooden boards that cut off the water, letting it in when they were lifted
- paths around the edges
- bridges so that farmers could move around easily.

The seasons

There were three seasons along the River Nile. The **inundation** was when the river flooded. This lasted from July to October. Then came the planting season, from November to April. May and June were harvest months and were very busy. The fully grown **crops** had to be cut down and removed before the Nile flooded again, so the farmers kept an anxious eye on the river.

Many people – especially important ones with time to spare – used the Nile for pleasure all year round. This man is hunting wild birds in the marshes along the riverbanks. He is using a small boat made from **papyrus reeds**.

During the inundation, farmers could not work in the fields. They spent some time mending their tools and looking after their animals. They also had to do **duty work** for the **pharaoh**. This was a set number of days of work that most people had to do. Some people paid others to do the work for them. Ordinary farmers could not afford to do this.

Scribes worked for the pharaoh all the time, so they did not have to do duty work. They kept records of everything, including the amount of **grain** collected during the harvest season on each piece of land as shown here.

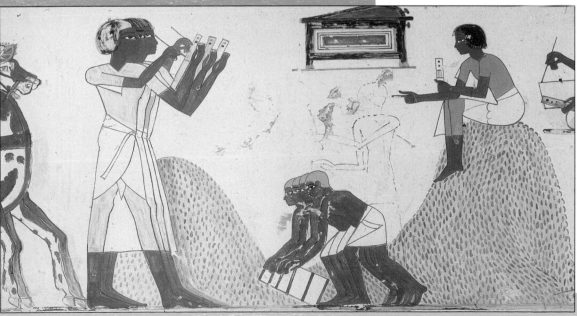

Farming

The people of ancient Egypt grew everything they needed to eat. The most important **crop** was **grain**, mostly barley and wheat. The ancient Egyptians used grain to make bread, porridge and beer. Grain was the first crop the farmers grew after the **inundation**. Once this was harvested, they grew vegetables – mainly onions, leeks, cabbages, beans, cucumbers and lettuce.

The ancient Egyptians used simple wooden farming tools. Tools used for cutting things, like the sickle in this picture, had cutting 'teeth' made from sharpened stone or copper.

Farmers planted fruit trees and vines along paths, to give shade as well as fruit. Dates, figs, pomegranates and grapes all grew well in the heat. Farmers kept bees, too. Honey was an important food, because the ancient Egyptians did not have sugar. Honey and dates were used to sweeten drinks and food.

ANIMALS

Cattle pulled the ploughs, and sheep and goats trod the seeds into the soil and ate the stalks of grain after the harvest. These animals were also useful for milk, cheese and meat. Ducks and geese were kept for eggs and meat, while bees were kept for honey

Farmers sometimes ploughed the soil using small wooden hand ploughs. Bigger ploughs were pulled by oxen, as shown in this ancient Egyptian tomb model.

Fishing

Ordinary ancient Egyptians did not eat much other meat, but they ate a lot of fish. The River Nile was full of all kinds of fish, such as catfish and eels. Small fishing boats were lightweight. They were made out of bundles of **papyrus reeds** tied together with rope. The fishermen had to be very careful moving about in the boats, so as not to overturn them.

The ancient Egyptians often have paintings of fishing on the walls of their tombs. Because these paintings show the perfect world of the **afterlife**, their nets are always full of huge fish! This painting shows a large wooden fishing boat.

We know that some ancient Egyptians went fishing with poles that had fishing lines with bone or bronze hooks on the end. They caught only one fish at a time this way. A better way to fish was to take out two boats, with a net slung between them. Fish got caught in the net. The catch had to be shared out between all the fishermen, but there was plenty of fish.

BEWARE, CROCS!

The Nile was full of crocodiles as well as fish. Fishermen must have been in constant fear of crocodiles. A **scribe** wrote about fishermen: 'Even if they get a good catch of fish, they still call out, blinded by fear, "the crocodile's waiting!"'

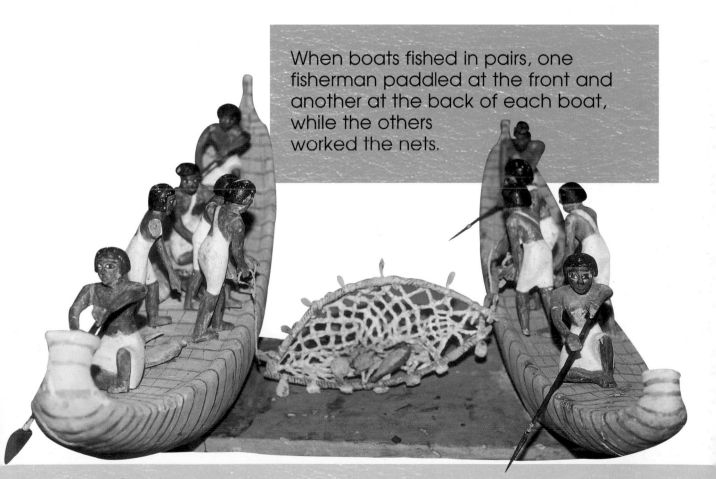

When boats fished in pairs, one fisherman paddled at the front and another at the back of each boat, while the others worked the nets.

Boat-building

Ancient Egyptian **papyrus reed** boats did not have high sides so they were like rafts. The sailors used paddles to move the boats along. From about 3100 BC the ancient Egyptians began to use sails on the boats, so they could catch the wind and use it to move faster. They still used papyrus reed boats for fishing.

TOOLS

The ancient Egyptians built papyrus boats using nothing but their hands. They built wooden boats using simple axes and saws with copper blades.

The ancient Egyptians could sail a wooden boat from Memphis to Elephantine in about seven days, with their sails up, using the wind. This was a trip of about 700 kilometres (430 miles). The journey back, against the wind, took about twelve days.

The boat-builders then made wooden boats from acacia trees, which grew well in the hot, dry weather. They used planks of wood that overlapped each other, tied together with rope. After about 2700 BC, the ancient Egyptians traded with other countries for cedar wood, which gave much larger planks.

Wooden boats like this one were better than papyrus boats because:
- they were stronger
- the planks could be built up to make sides
- they were more waterproof
- they lasted longer
- they were better for long journeys
- there was more space for the sailors.

Trade

The first people to live in ancient Egypt traded from village to village, swapping food, clothes, pots and baskets with each other. They did not travel far to trade, or trade with other countries. In about 3100 BC, Egypt began to be ruled by one ruler, the **pharaoh**. Other countries saw it become a powerful, organized country. They began to want to trade with Egypt.

Things brought in from other countries were mostly expensive, for example perfume, wood, silver, jewels and even animals, such as giraffes. This silver cup came from Greece.

The ancient Egyptians used the Nile to carry trade goods as much as they could. **Traders** sometimes used small **papyrus reed** boats to ferry goods short distances. They used wooden boats with sails for longer distances, or for goods that took up a lot of space. When they had to carry goods across the desert, they used donkeys. The goods were packed in baskets slung over the animal's back. In ancient times, there were very few camels in Egypt to use for transport.

If the Nile did not flood much one year, there was less soil to grow **crops** in. So people had less **grain** at harvest time and the pharaoh had to trade for grain from other countries. **Scribes** measured how much grain was put in and taken out of grain stores, as shown in this picture.

17

Ancient Egyptian houses were made from mud bricks. Important people lived in the biggest houses. They had bathrooms where they poured river water over themselves to wash. The water drained away through a hole in the floor. For toilets, they used buckets with wooden seats, which were washed out with water and emptied on the fields. Ordinary people just used the fields as toilets and washed in the river.

Some houses, like this one, were built on a mud-brick platform instead of directly on the ground. This was probably in case of very high water levels when the River Nile rose in the **inundation.**

18

Most ancient Egyptians did not have much furniture, or many possessions. Most people had wooden beds, but poorer people slept on a mud-brick platform instead. They had stools for sitting on, and one or more small, low tables. Folding stools and tables could be carried to and from the roof more easily.

GARDENS

Because Egypt was so hot and dry, gardens were not common. Water for them had to be brought from the river. Important people had gardens with ponds, which they filled with fish and ducks. They grew trees that gave shade and food, like date palms and pomegranate trees.

Among the possessions buried with ancient Egyptians were models of their houses. This model shows the doorway, window and courtyard of a house.

Clothes and make-up

The ancient Egyptians wore as little as possible, because of the heat. Fishermen just wore a short piece of cloth wrapped round the waist. Women wore a **tunic**. Young children often wore nothing at all. Ancient Egyptians' skin was not likely to burn, but people did get very hot. This is one reason why they kept their hair short, or even shaved it all off.

People wore wigs made from human hair or, if they could not afford this, plants. One ancient Egyptian wig, like this one, has been found that still had the head lice in it from the person whose hair was used to make it!

LAUNDRY

Most people had their washing done for them, as homes did not have running water. Washing was done in the River Nile. Men, not women, did the laundry. Crocodile attack was always a danger around the river.

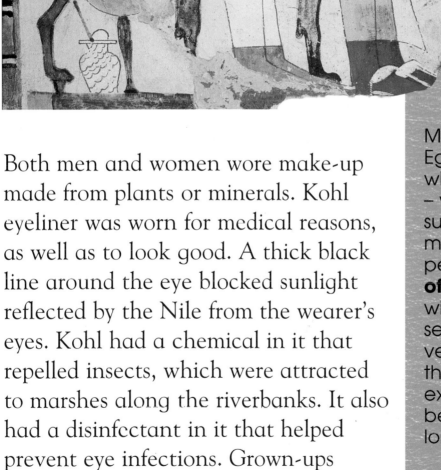

Both men and women wore make-up made from plants or minerals. Kohl eyeliner was worn for medical reasons, as well as to look good. A thick black line around the eye blocked sunlight reflected by the Nile from the wearer's eyes. Kohl had a chemical in it that repelled insects, which were attracted to marshes along the riverbanks. It also had a disinfectant in it that helped prevent eye infections. Grown-ups often wore perfume, too. It was mixed into fat that was put on their wigs.

Most ancient Egyptians wore white clothes – white reflects sunlight the most. Important people, like this **official** and his wife, wore several layers of very thin cloth that was more expensive because it took longer to make.

Estates

In ancient Egypt, all the land belonged to the **pharaoh**. He kept some land for himself. He divided up the rest into large areas called estates. Each estate was run by an **official** or a **temple**. The estates were expected to give the pharaoh a share of all their animals, **crops** and the goods their workers produced. Ordinary people could not own land. They worked a piece of land on an estate.

On this small estate there was:
- a big house for the family that ran the estate
- a garden for the family
- store rooms
- workshops
- homes for the servants
- stables for the horses (not visible)
- a wall around all of this
- farmland between the estate and the Nile.

store rooms

garden

farmland

family house

workshops

wall

servants' homes

Once a year, all the animals on an estate were brought together and counted. This tomb model shows a cattle count. People were rewarded or punished depending on the health of their animals and how many young ones they had produced.

Scribes on the estate kept records of everything: how much seed was planted, how much **grain** was grown, how many animals there were. The pharaoh could ask for this information at any time. Estates had their own stores for grain from the harvest each year, and gave it out to the workers each week. Some of the grain was saved to use as seed the next year.

ALL YOU NEED

Estates were not just big houses with farmland attached. Most of them had their own workshops that made everything that anyone on the estate needed. So they had workers making cooking pots, shoes and cloth.

The ancient Egyptians believed in many gods and goddesses. Some gods, like Amun, were worshipped all over Egypt. Others were worshipped in just one place, or by some people more than others. Fishermen worshipped Sobek, the crocodile god, hoping he would keep them safe from the crocodiles in the Nile. Hapy was the god of the Nile. Hymns were written to him.

These amulets show Sobek, the crocodile god. Ancient Egyptians wore amulets to keep them safe from danger, but these have no holes for a string to tie them on. They were probably buried with a dead person, so they could have Sobek's protection in the **afterlife**.

Temples were built as homes for statues of the gods and goddesses, and places to leave them offerings. They were not buildings for ordinary people to worship in. Ordinary people often only went to temples for yearly **religious festivals**, when the statues were taken out for everyone to see. At other times, the people worshipped at **shrines** set up along the riverbank, or in their own homes. Shrines were often just a small mud-brick altar, with a shelf to leave an offering.

Priests were very important in preparing the dead for the afterlife. This painting shows priests praying in front of a mummy in his case before it was put in its tomb.

Funerals

The River Nile was important in preparing bodies for burial and often in the **funeral ceremony**. The ancient Egyptians believed the dead came back to life. So they preserved their bodies and buried them with many possessions. They did the preserving, called embalming, in open-sided tents down by the river. The river provided water to wash the bodies and for the 'purification' ritual during embalming. The breeze from the river carried away the smell of the chemicals used.

Water was important in many of the stages of burial, to purify the body. In this painting, one priest, in a jackal mask, holds up the mummy case while another priest sprinkles water at it.

Cemeteries were often on the opposite side of the River Nile to the towns and villages where people lived. People did not like living too close to the dead, but they wanted to visit the cemeteries often, to pray to their lost relatives and friends and bring them gifts. The ancient Egyptians did not build bridges across the Nile, so there was always a ferry that ran between the cemeteries and the places on the other bank.

Family members accompanied the body of a dead relative by ferry boat across the Nile to the cemetery, as shown in this ancient Egyptian tomb model.

Food

The ancient Egyptians did all their cooking out of doors. Bread was cooked in special ovens. Almost everything else was cooked in pots over an open fire, either on the mud-brick roof or in a courtyard. People ate out of doors, too. They ate their main meal in the cool of the evening. At breakfast and lunch they mostly ate bread with vegetables or cheese.

This tomb model shows servants brewing, baking and butchering meat in the kitchen of an estate. These jobs were not actually done in the same place, at the same time.

Egyptian recipe – flat bread

This bread has to stand to rise for about two hours between mixing up and baking. You can leave it alone for this time. WARNING: Ask an adult to help you with the cooking.

1 Dissolve the yeast in 2 tablespoons of the warm water. Add a pinch of sugar. Leave until frothy (10 minutes).

2 Mix the salt and flour in a bowl.

3 Pour the yeast mix into the flour. Mix with your hands. Add more warm water, slowly, until you have a squishy dough. Push and fold the dough (add flour if it gets sticky) until smooth and a bit stretchy.

4 Put a little oil on your hands. Roll the dough in it, replace in the bowl and cover with a cloth. Leave in a warm place for 2 hours. The dough grows to twice its size.

5 Push and fold the dough again. It loses air and gets smaller. Break it into pieces the size of a small orange.

6 Turn the oven on as high as it will go.

7 Flatten the dough pieces on a floured board until about 8 mm thick. Put on an oiled tray, cover and leave for 20 minutes. Once risen, cook the breads in the oven for about 8 minutes.

Egyptian people still live along the banks of the River Nile. In some ways, their lives are the same as their ancestors'. For example, some farmers still use a *shaduf* to lift water from the **irrigation canals**. There is one way in which life is very different. In 1902 a dam was built at Aswan, to control the flooding of the Nile. Since then, the flow of the Nile has been regulated, so that the land can be watered and **crops** grown throughout the year.

Modern Egyptians use many different kinds of boats on the River Nile. *Feluccas*, like this one, are similar in design to the small wooden boats used by the ancient Egyptians.

Glossary

afterlife imaginary world, where life was pleasant, to which ancient Egyptians believed they went after death

archaeologist person who uncovers old buildings and burial sites to find out about the past

cemetery place where dead people are buried

crops plants that farmers grow for food or to make material for such things as cloth and baskets

duty work set number of days each year that people had to work for the pharaoh. Scribes did not have to do this work, but everyone else did.

funeral ceremony rituals that are done when a dead person is buried

grain several types of grasses, all with fat seeds that can be eaten. Barley, wheat and oats are all grain.

inundation time when the River Nile flooded its banks

irrigation canal ditch dug to carry water from one place to another

officials people who help to run a country

papyrus reeds tall thin plants that grow by the River Nile

pharaoh ruler of ancient Egypt

religious ceremony/festival special time or event when people go to one place to pray to a god or goddess

reservoir specially dug pond where water is stored

scribes the only people in ancient Egypt who could read or write

shrine place where ancient Egyptians came to pray to gods and goddesses and leave them gifts

temple place where people pray to gods and goddesses

trader person who buys and sells or swaps things that other people have made, sometimes bringing them from far away

tunic T-shirt-shaped clothing that came to at least just above the knee, worn by men women and children

More books to read

Ancient Egypt: Builders and Craftsmen, Jane Shuter (Heinemann Library, 1999)

Ancient Egypt: Farming and Food, Jane Shuter (Heinemann Library, 1998)

Ancient Egyptian Children, Richard Thames (Heinemann Library, 2002)

Ancient Egyptian Homes, Brenda Williams (Heinemann Library, 2002)

Index